from UNINCORPORATED TERRITORY

[guma']

ALSO BY CRAIG SANTOS PEREZ

from UNINCORPORATED TERRITORY [HACHA]
Tinfish Press, 2008

from UNINCORPORATED TERRITORY [SAINA]
Omnidawn Publishing, 2010

from UNINCORPORATED TERRITORY

[guma']

CRAIG SANTOS PEREZ

OMNIDAWN PUBLISHING
RICHMOND, CALIFORNIA
2014

Saina Ma'ase to Florence Taitague and everyone at the
Guam Public Library for their permission to reprint archival
images on the cover of this book.

Cover photograph by James R. Evans, USN

Book cover & interior design by Cassandra Smith

Offset printed in the United States
by Edwards Brothers Malloy, Ann Arbor, Michigan
on 55# Enviro Natural, 100% recycled, 100% PCW
Acid Free Archival Quality FSC Certified Paper
with Rainbow FSC Certified Colored End Papers

Library of Congress Cataloging-in-Publication Data

Santos Perez, Craig.
  [Poems. Selections]
From unincorporated territory [guma'] / Craig Santos Perez.
    pages cm
  ISBN 978-1-890650-91-9 (Trade Paperback : alk. paper)
  1. Guam--Poetry. I. Title.
  PS3619.A598A6 2014
  811'.6--dc23

                                    2013045798

Published by Omnidawn Publishing, Richmond, California
www.omnidawn.com   (510) 237-5472   (800) 792-4957
            10 9 8 7 6 5 4 3 2 1
            ISBN: 978-1-890650-91-9

~

hanom www.save hanom pagan.org hanom

~

MAP OF CONTENTS

‑

~

~

~

[MATTIYU] ::

:: [HAMMERSTONE]

from the legends of juan malo *[a malologue]*

～

...maps emerging out of the Pacific, maps brought in and imposed, maps combining the two, maps which are deliberate erasures and replacements; maps which reveal the rivers, mountains and geography of a people's agaga/psyche; maps used to perpetuate fictions/myths about ourselves; new maps, new fusions and interweavings...

—Albert Wendt *from* "Pacific Maps and Fiction(s): A Personal Journey" (1991)

～

Guam is "Where America's Day Begins." Guam is the "westernmost furthest forward sovereign US territory in the Pacific." Guam is a non-self-governing colony. Guam is a US citizen ever since the 1950 Organic Act. Guam is part of the US Postal System (GU, 96910-96932). Guam "reps" the "671." Guam is a duty-free port outside the US Customs Zone. Guam is expected to homeport the Pacific fleet. Guam is an acronym for "Give Us American Military." Guam is a pivot point in a realignment of US forces in the Pacific. Guam is a target. Guam is America's front porch to Asia. Guam is a mini Hawai'i. Guam is strategically invisible. Guam is published by the Guam Hotel & Restaurant Association and the Guam Visitors Bureau. Guam is a beach for sunburnt tourists in bikinis. Guam is an acronym for "Give Us Asian Money." Guam is air-conditioned. Guam is updating its Facebook status. Guam is a punch line in Hollywood movie jokes. Guam is being used to film three Hollywood Movies in the coming years. Guam is learning English as a Colonial Language (ECL). Guam is frequent flyer miles. Guam is endangered. Guam is one of [our] most curious possessions. Guam is no longer "Guam."

ginen tidelands *[latte stone park] [hagåtña, guåhan]*

[for my dad]

⁓

The fallen Latte *is the sign. It is from within the row of* Latte *that we feel our strength. It is the severed capstone that gives us Their message,* "Ti monhayon I che'cho." *We will not rest until the* Latte *is whole.*

—Cecilia C. T. Perez *from* "Signs of Being: A Chamoru Spiritual Journey" (1997)

⁓

i haligi
a pillar

i tasa
a capstone

i tataotao
a body

⁓

his hands—
husk coconut—

cooks and
feeds [us]—

stories—*this*
raised house—

⁓

at quarry
outline forms

to sing
forward—carve

limestone *to*
sing past—

citizen : drafted
vietnam war—

the rifle
he kept—

his uniform
his fatigue

soak coconut
fibers—dry

under sun—
"make rope"

braided hair—
"like this"

hålla haligi—
pull sky—

hålla tasa—
"pull, son"

with [our]
entire breath

[our] bones :
acho' latte

removed from—
to museum

of trespass—
to here—

ginen (sub)aerial roots *[13° 28' 0" N / 144° 46' 59" E]*

⁓

Curiously, there are no known migration legends in Chamorro lore...

—Robert Tenorio Torres *from* "Pre-Contact Marianas Folklore, Legends, and Literature" (2003)

⁓

I've never been able to write a poem about the day *from indicates a particular time or place as a starting point* my family left Guåhan *[we] have*. As years passed, details faded *from refers to a specific location as the first of two limits*. Who came to the airport to say good-bye? What did I carry *from imagines a cause an agent an instrument a source or an origin* in my luggage? What was left behind?

European maps from the 15th century represented the Pacific Ocean as an empty space *from marks borders removal or exclusion* separating Asia and America. With Europe at the center, Oceania was halved *of trespass* on the margins of the map. Guåhan has been given many names *instill ownership* over the last four centuries—*from* Spain: "Islas de las Velas Latinas" (Island of Lateen Sails) and "Islas de los Ladrones" (Island of the Thieves)—*from* Japan: "Omiya Jima" (Great Shrine Island)—*from* the US: "Guam"—*lisiensan dog ga'lago tag*

In "Bittersweet Memories," Chamorro writer Helen Perez narrates her childhood growing up in 1960s Virginia, where her military father was stationed: "One day in our geography class, my teacher taped several maps on the wall and asked each of us to stand in front of the class and mark where our parents and grandparents were born. I tried to remember everything my mom told me about Guam. I only remembered that she told me it would be hard to find on a map unless I looked very closely and carefully, because it was so small. She said it's in the Pacific Ocean, and it's a tiny dot on the map, so find the Philippine Islands first because it's not far from there...I knelt down so I could see better and found the Philippine Islands. I still couldn't find Guam and I started crying because everyone was waiting for their turn, and I was taking so long. I only saw a cluster of islands called 'Micronesian Islands,' but my mom never mentioned those islands to me. I looked at my teacher and said, 'Please help me find Guam.'"

~

Latte, or *latde*, are stone structures composed of two parts: a haligi (vertical pillar) and a tasa (bowl-shaped capstone) *the fallen latte is the sign.* The haligi—carved from limestone, basalt, or sandstone—ranges in height from three to nine feet and is wide at the base *bullets ricochet* and narrow towards the top. The tasa, made from inverted coral head or carved from limestone, sits atop the haligi *this raised house to sing.* Completed latte structures *gives us their message* were arranged in parallel rows of at least four pairs evenly spaced. They formed the foundations of homes, schools, canoe shelters, food sheds, and communal spaces *momongmong*

Timbers and coconut fiber *first-person singular [gumå'-hu: my house]* were used to create a floor *first-person plural [guma'-måmi]* and A-frame dwelling structure atop the latte stones *second-person singular [gumå'-mu].* The roof was thatched from palm leaves, pandanus, or sword grass *second-person plural [guma'-miyu].* Archaeologists have found an estimated 270 latte sites *third-person singular [gumå'-ña: her/his house]* on Guåhan, dating the beginning of latte construction at AD 900 *third-person plural [guma'-ñiha].* Bones have been found buried beneath the *second-person inclusive plural [gumå'-ta: our house]* sheltered space of the raised house *with [our] entire breath hunggan hunggan hunggan magahet*

ginen **sounding lines** *[date : 8/8/93][epicenter : 12.982° n*
144.801° e] [depth : 59 km] [strength : 8.2]

remember just
at dinner

the power
goes out—

a length of
rope—plummet—

mom lights
candles—

scoops
|us| rice—

dad care
-fully por-

tions fish
onto [our]

plates—*sea*
floor

sonar—pull
sounding lines—

knots tie
each end—

sudden
quakes—

[we] run
under doorway—

pictures
fall and

break—
memories

thread
fathoms of

water—
when light

returns
pieces of

glass
shimmering

fish
carcass—

~

At the present moment I see no chance whatever of breaking into official circles and discussing with his Excellency my proposals for PEACE in the Pacific....I should quite plainly propose to give Guam to the Japanese in return for one set of color and sound films of the 300 best Noh dramas. The films could not be delivered all at once, so we would not need to give up Guam all at once....You may think I am joking about this Guam proposition. I am not. I ask the impartial auditor whether the individual American citizen wouldn't get a great deal MORE out of a set of such films as I saw, the one I saw in Washington two years ago, than he would out of a few tons of tungsten, with possibly a few family coffins thrown in. It would mean, and I admit it would mean, getting educated up to the point of knowing what is meant by Kumasaka and Kagekiyo. The film I saw was of Awoi no Uye. The Japanese would be truly grateful to us, not for Guam, but for prodding 'em on to make a complete high grade record of these plays before the tradition gets damaged.

—Ezra Pound *from* Ezra Pound Speaking: Radio Speeches of World War II (1978)

~

"hu hongge
i lina'la' tataotao
ta'lo åmen"

~

My family migrated *removed* from Guåhan *[we] have* to California in 1995, when I was a sophomore in high school. One of the reasons my parents decided to move was so that I could be *born and fed and grows and* better prepared to succeed in a "mainland" university. Not knowing how [we] would pay for college, I attended the Army recruiter's presentation *aim target island* at my new high school. The recruiter wore his uniform *what does not change* with pride; he reminded me of my relatives who were in the military. When he said the Army would pay for college, he answered my prayers *bullets fragment and*

About a month later, he visited the house my family was renting. "I don't even think we let him in the house. I just think we talked to him through the screen door," my mom says over the phone when I call her to ask if she remembers the day the recruiter came. "I didn't want you joining the service because I don't believe in fighting wars or having to go off to fight wars when you were so young. You didn't even have a chance to live yet. I don't think it's fair that they recruit kids at such a young age. I don't even think they should be allowed on the high school campus. I want to see those young kids have a chance to grow and live. I know a lot of kids were joining the service because a lot of people can't afford to go to college. But I wanted us to find a different way. Thank god you never joined."

She hands the phone to my dad *his fatigues*: "I don't like that he came to our house to recruit. He even came in his uniform. And when he found out I was a veteran and I was in the Army, he thought that was good. But I don't want anyone else in the family going to the military. He was trying to tell me that when you graduate you can get money to go to college. I always thought, what if you don't live? You went and you die and you don't get any college then. I could see a guy like that is just trying to make his quota as a recruiter. They think parents will be naïve, and they say that you don't have to worry about college and that you can travel all around the world, get free clothes, free food and housing. But you have to look beyond. You don't have to go to the military."

―

I attended a university in California with scholarships, loans *a cage can be either solid material wire mesh or*, work-study, and my parents' help. For the semester abroad, I studied Italian Renaissance art and literature in Florence, Italy. I was in Beginning Italian Language class on September 11, 2001, when [we] heard the news. I followed other students to an English pub to watch the BBC. The newscaster compared the attack on the World Trade Center to the attack on Pearl Harbor *and ricochet*

On December 8, 1941, Japan bombed Guåhan—a US territorial possession since 1898. That day *bodies falling from* many residents were attending mass to commemorate the Feast of the Immaculate Conception, honoring [our] patron saint, Santa Marian Kamalen. Two days later, Japan invaded Guam and conquered the US military forces *towers falling from*

On September 12, 2001, I attended a candlelight vigil near the Duomo for the victims. I was 21 years old *momongmong*

⏜

*"i believe
i lina'la' tataotao
ta'lo, åmen"*

⏜

The US invaded *when snakes arrive* Afghanistan on October 7, 2001. I hated showing my passport on trains as I traveled in Europe. I explained over and over: "I am not American," even though I speak English like an American, even though I am a US citizen *this cage can be either solid material wire mesh or*. I explained over and over where and what "Guam" is.

The US *sliding along the passages* invaded Iraq on March 20, 2003. The first Chamorro soldier died in Iraq on December 8, 2003. *Christopher Rivera Wesley.* He was 26 years old.

Chamorros *removed from* enlist in the US armed forces at alarmingly high rates. Military recruiters based in Guam almost always exceed their quotas. Headline: "US Territories : A Recruiter's Paradise : Army Goes Where Fish Are Biting"—

ginen the micronesian kingfisher *[i sihek]*

⁓

[our] nightmare : no
birdsong—
the jungle was riven emptied
of *[i sihek]* bright blue green turquoise red gold
feathers—everywhere : brown
tree snakes avian
silence—

the snakes entered
without words when [we] saw them it was too late—
they were at [our] doors sliding along
the passages of *[i sihek]*
empire—then

the zookeepers came—
called it *species survival plan*—captured *[i sihek]* and transferred
the last
twenty-nine micronesian kingfishers
to zoos for captive breeding *[1988]*—they repeated *[i sihek]*
and repeated :

"if it weren't for us
your birds   *[i sihek]*
would be gone
forever"

what does not change /

last wild seen—

DEIS Public Comment : "This is a huge document to digest"

DEIS Public Comment : "It doesn't matter what we gain from the buildup; it's what we lose

DEIS Public Comment : "Buenas. First off, thank you for the false sense of participation created by the comment period. The opportunity to vent, while completely meaningless, is at very least cathartic"

DEIS Public Comment : "The destruction of the land is a sign of disrespect to our ancestors"

DEIS Public Comment : "How much sewage and solid waste can our island expect?"

> —*Many comments address how full of _____ our colonizer is, but the real concern was where our colonizer was going to put all that _____, especially with 80,000 more ___holes coming to Guam*

DEIS Public Comment : "Military peeps please hear me clearly. I don't want no trouble but just believe me things will go down if you mess up. Just don't start no bull like on Okinawa. Guåhan soldier for life"

> —*Craig! Had my students comment in class one day and I received a torn paper, with red ink and large letters that said: FUH-Q MILITARY. Then a tiny little post-it attached that said "Sorry, That's all I could think of because I'm really mad"*

DEIS Public Comment : "Where are the comments to these issues sent? Who sees them? Will the public see any of these comments?"

ginen the legends of juan malo *[a malologue]*

⁓

It was a theory of mine that former cannibals of Oceania now feasted on Spam because Spam came the nearest to approximating the porky taste of human flesh....It was a fact that the people-eaters of the Pacific had all evolved, or perhaps degenerated, into Spam-eaters.

—Paul Theroux *from* The Happy Isles of Oceania: Paddling the Pacific (2006)

⁓

Guam is considered the SPAM® capital of the world. On average, each Chamorro consumes 16 tins of SPAM® each year, which is more per capita than any other country. Headline: Guam Struggles to Find Its Roots From Beneath SPAM®'s Carbon Footprint. Do all seven McDonald's restaurants on Guam feature SPAM® on the menu? Welcome to Guam, let [us] present you with the gourmet luxury of SPAM® at your birthday, wedding, and funeral. A culinary legacy of American troops stationed in the Pacific during World War II, SPAM® is also popular in Hawai'i, the Philippines, Okinawa, and South Korea (and all places with a history of US military presence). In fact, SPAM® may have been responsible for Hitler's defeat; the Allies would have starved without SPAM®. Plus, it's processed so I guess [we] can save it for the coming war between the US and China, right? Wow, I haven't seen this much SPAM® since I lived on Guam and the car dealership there started offering a 50lb bag of imported white rice and a case of SPAM® with every car purchase. In the devastating wake of Typhoon Omar, Hormel donated 40,000 cases of SPAM® to the Salvation Army's disaster relief effort. The end result of so much SPAM® can be found in [our] newspaper's obituary pages.

DEIS Public Comment : "My main reason for being against the military buildup is for what happened in Okinawa. A girl got raped"

DEIS Public Comment : "The lives of the native ocean inhabitants are more important than a parking lot for war ships"

DEIS Public Comment : "They can't even pronounce the names of the villages right for God's sake!"

—Pronunciation before colonization!

DEIS Public Comment : "On behalf of the outrigger Guam Resort, OHANA Bayview Guam and OHANA Oceanview Guam representing a combined total of 939 rooms and almost 350 employees, I hereby submit testimony in support. The buildup will offer our industry an increase in the number of visitors and additional customer diversity"

DEIS Public Comment : "This bothers me so much that I am typing this response at midnight with my cellphone"

DEIS Public Comment : "I don't think I'm allowed to say that I'm against the military buildup because both of my parents are for the build up, and my dad is in the Air Force"

ginen the legends of juan malo *[a malologue]*

Rub the entire block of SPAM•, along with the accompanying gelatinous goo, onto your wood furniture. The oils from the SPAM• moisturize the wood and give it a nice luster. Plus, you'll have enough left over to use as your own personal lubricant (a true Pacific dinner date). Why didn't you tell me about the "In Honor of Guam's Liberation" SPAM•! I'm trying to collect them all! Once I was on a diet and SPAM• faded from my consciousness. Then I met my future wife, who's Hawaiian, and SPAM• became part of my life again (a true Pacific romance). Maybe the economic downturn will help people appreciate SPAM• instead of loathing it. SPAM• doesn't have to be unhealthy; I eat SPAM• every day and I'm not dead, yet—just switch to SPAM• Lite. Despite rumors, SPAM• is NOT made of such odds and ends as hooves, ears, brains, native peoples, or whole baby pigs. The name itself stands for *Specially Processed Army Meal, Salted Pork And More, Super Pink Artificial Meat, Snake Possum And Mongoose,* or *Some People Are Missing*. My uncle is the reigning Guam SPAM• king. He won the last SPAM• cook off with his Spicy SPAM• meatballs. I will never forget the two-pound SPAM• bust of George Washington he made for Liberation Day, toasted crispy on the outside with raw egg yolk in the hollow center— the kids loved it! Only a fool would start a company in Guam that provides SPAM• protection. For Xmas, I bought a snow globe featuring a can of SPAM• sitting on an island. Turn it over and a typhoon swirls madly, unable to unseat SPAM• from its place of honor. I have a souvenir can I bought after seeing Monty Python's SPAM•ALOT on Broadway in New York City. It cost me $10 and is the most expensive SPAM• I've ever bought. I will never eat it.

[GUADDUKON] ::

:: [ADZES]

ginen the micronesian kingfisher *[i sihek]*

⌐

exterior features : quarter inch plywood
screened mesh cage front *[i sihek]* with bumpers
and burlap shield—

⌐

"a rare micronesian kingfisher chick, weighing five grams,
hatched at the national zoo's conservation and research center
[2004] [i sihek]

⌐

interior ceiling : foam rubber or burlap stuffed
with straw—external minimum size :
nine inch by nine inch—internal height : minimum ten inch
clearance between floor and ceiling padding—
perching : *[i sihek]* half inch diameter—

⌐

"our newest pair of micronesian kingfishers at the san diego
zoo is currently raising a chick *[2007] [i sihek]*

⌐

the minimum enclosure
size for breeding pairs : ten feet by eight feet
with a height of ten feet containment—
this cage *[i sihek]*
can be either solid material wire mesh or glass—
on these displays *[i sihek]*

what does not change / is

is born and fed and grows and dies—

ginen ta(la)ya

⌣

[2004]

{U.S. Army 1st Lt. Michael Aguon Vega, 42, a Guam native, died after he sustained injuries from a roadside blast in Iraq}

{U.S. Army Sgt. Yihjyh "Eddie" Lang Chen, 31, of Saipan was killed in Iraq when his unit was attacked}

{U.S. Marine Cpl. JayGee Meluat, 24, a native of Palau, was killed by enemy fire in Iraq}

{U.S. Army Sgt. Skipper Soram, 23, from Kolonia, in the FSM state of Pohnpei, died after an explosion occurred near his security post in Iraq}

{Ferdinand Ibabao, an employee of DynCorp security company, was killed in an explosion in Iraq. Ibabao had been a Guam police officer. He was 36}

{U.S. Army Spc. Jonathan Pangelinan Santos, a former Santa Rita resident, was killed in Iraq, when his vehicle hit a land mine. He was 22}

⌣

> *"hu hongge*
> *the life tataotao*
> *ta'lo åmen"*

⌣

In 2005, I sit *algae mats and fronds* across from my grandfather on a small kitchen table in his apartment in Fairfield, California. He talks story about growing up in Guåhan *[we] have* and how he was taught to weave a talaya, or throw net. Threads hung from hooks in the ceiling, lead weights at the end of each thread *hacha hugua tulu fatfat lima*. "You hold the nicho like this," he says. "And the nasa around your fingers like this." He points to the empty ceiling: "The size of the fish determines the size of the mesh." He stands *ghost nets*

and cradles his imaginary talaya in his hands and bends his body *coral bones* into proper form. He refers to the mesh of the net as "eyes" *these passages my sourcing*. He uncoils and throws the talaya directly over me. He picks up the net and stalks through the kitchen. He explains how you can identify a fish by reading the surface movement *where fish are hiding* of currents and shadows. How to minimize your shadow depending on the angle of the sun *"pull, son"*

After a few casts, he seems surprised that his hands are empty. He remembers holding his niece's hands as they walk down San Roman hill towards the Dulce Nombre de Maria Cathedral-Basilica in Hagåtña to celebrate the Feast of the Immaculate Conception. December 8, 1941. He is 15 years old *bullets fragment*. "During mass we heard a bunch of planes...we could hear the bombing and the priest announced that mass is ended" *and ricochet*

A few days later he walks with everyone from his village to be processed *caged within [our] disappearance* at the military checkpoint in Plaza de España. "I remember seeing for the first time the Japanese flag," he says. "Sentries were posted and beat those who didn't bow to them. We waited in line and they gave us a white piece of cloth with Japanese writing on it and we had to keep it pinned there"—he points to my chest—"by our heart

and they pointed to the sky
where we had to bow." He stands *with [our] entire breath* and straightens his body and straightens his arms against his sides as he looks straight past me. He *is born and fed and grows and* bows.

They force him and others to build the airstrip in Barrigada. "It took us six months to cut out the hill to fill in the airstrip. Their bayonets in our backs." He was then stationed in Asan to construct machine gun encampments *bullets fragment and*

First, they make the forms, mixing salt water from the beach with cement and sand *this cage can be either solid material wire mesh or*. "I never carved my initials into the concrete," he says. "I even tried to avoid leaving fingerprints."

~

[2005]

~~[U.S. Army Staff Sgt. Steven Bayow, 42, a Yap native, was killed in Iraq when a bomb hit their vehicle]~~

~~[U.S. Army Spc. Derence Jack, 31, of Saipan was killed in a roadside bomb attack in Iraq]~~

~~[U.S. Army Sgt. Wilgene Lieto, 28, of Saipan was killed in a roadside bomb attack in Iraq]~~

~~[U.S. Army Spc. Richard DeGracia Naputi Jr., 24, of Talofofo was killed in Iraq when a homemade bomb detonated during combat operations]~~

~

*"hu hongge
i lina'la' body
ta'lo åmen"*

~

On July 21, 1944, the US military invaded Guåhan and *the jungle was riven* a three-week battle for the island ensued. Japan surrendered. A year later, this date was celebrated as "Liberation Day" with a religious procession centering around Santa Marian Kamalen. Parades, marching bands, floats, games, and a carnival were added over the years *to pledge allegiance*. Young women sell fundraising tickets to become the next Liberation Day Queen. They say this is a time *when fish are dying* for Chamorros to express [our] loyalty and gratitude to the US. They say that [we] enlist in the military at such high rates to pay the debt of liberation.

[2006]

[U.S. Army Pfc. Kasper Allen Camacho Dudkiewicz, 23, of Chalan Pago was killed in Iraq, when the Humvee in which he was the gunner was involved in a vehicle collision]

[U.S. Army Pfc. Henry Paul, 24, of Kolonia, in the FSM state of Pohnpei died in Baghdad of injuries sustained when their M2A3 Bradley Fighting Vehicle rolled over]

[U.S. Army Sgt. Jesse Castro, 22, a Guam native, was killed when a roadside explosion destroyed their Humvee in Iraq]

"hu hongge
i lina'la' tataotao
return åmen"

In 2005, the "US-Japan Roadmap for Realignment Implementation" was announced. This military buildup proposed the construction of facilities to house and support the transfer of 8,000 marines *their uniforms* from Okinawa to Guam, the establishment of an Air and Missile Defense Task Force, the building of a live firing range complex, and the creation of a deep-draft wharf in Apra Harbor to berth nuclear-powered aircraft carriers *of trespass*

[2007]

[U.S. Marine Cpl. Adam Quitugua Emul, 20, from Saipan, was killed while conducting combat operations in Iraq]

[U.S. Army Cpl. Lee Roy Apatang Camacho, 27, from Saipan died of wounds he sustained from an explosion in Iraq]

[Guam Army National Guard Sgt. ~~Gregory~~ D. Fejeran ~~was killed in Ethiopia when the vehicle he was in rolled over. He was 28~~]

[~~Guam Army National Guard Sgt.~~ Christopher Fernandez ~~was killed in Ethiopia when the vehicle he was in rolled over. He was 28~~]

[~~U.S. Army Spc.~~ John D. Flores~~, 21, of Barrigada, was killed when his unit came under attack by enemy fire in Iraq~~]

[~~U.S. Army Pfc.~~ Victor Michael Fontanilla~~, 23, was killed in a bomb blast in Iraq~~]

[~~U.S. Army Sgt.~~ Iosiwo Uruo ~~died in Iraq of wounds suffered when his unit came under attack by enemy forces. He was 27~~]

[~~U.S. Army Cpl.~~ Meresebang Ngiraked~~, 21, of Koror, Palau, died from injuries he sustained from a vehicle-based improvised explosive device in Iraq~~]

[~~Army Pfc.~~ Jose Charfauros Jr.~~, 33, of Rota was one of 14 soldiers killed in a single day in Iraq~~]

[~~Army Maj.~~ Henry Ofeciar ~~died when enemy forces using small arms fire and rocket-propelled grenades attacked his unit in Afghanistan. He was 37~~]

[~~Navy Master-at-Arms~~ Anamarie San Nicolas Camacho~~, 20, of Tinian and Guam, was killed in Bahrain~~]

"hu hongge
i lina'la' tataotao
ta'lo amen"

ginen sounding lines

remember just dad
tied an old tire to

a metal fence pole
so [we] could practice

pitching—*o say can you hear*
the hollow sound when

the baseball strikes
rubber—the rattling when

it strikes wire—or
that perfect sound—

speak onglish only
when [we] strike the pole

through the center of—*o*
say can you remember

just little league—barrigada
"tigers"—black and gold

uniforms—*red seams*—
my brother played for father

duenas memorial high school
"friars"—maroon and gold

uniforms—*to pledge allegiance*—
[we] collected american

baseball cards and cheered
for the "bash brothers"

in "oakland"—near where
brian moved for college *blue*

skies—the coliseum was
an island—green and

gold uniforms—*white*
bases—[we] stand

to sing the national
anthem—*o say*

can you see
[us]—*what follows*

your flag?

ginen (sub)aerial roots

Archaeologists *of trespass* mark the end of the "Latte Period" and the beginning of the "Historic Period" at AD 1521 when Magellan came. The Spanish burned houses and fell the latte stones. Every new voyage incorporated new data into new maps; every new voyage brought [us] a new storm—

George Anson, a British Navy commander, arrived in the Chamorro archipelago during his military circumnavigation in the 18th century. His ship's draftsman disassembled a Chamorro outrigger canoe to measure and draw its parts *enemy hands pull*. These canoes, once numerous, had nearly disappeared by the time Anson arrived because the Spanish military burned canoes to immobilize Chamorros and relocate [us] into Catholic parishes *this choked thing [we]*

In 1992, a group named Traditions About Seafaring Islands, or TASI, was founded in Guåhan *[we] have* to revive and perpetuate navigational practices, from canoe building to the reading of winds, waves, stars, and currents *with [our] entire breath*. In 2007, members of TASI built a sakman, a large outrigger canoe, with the aid of the Anson drawing and the guidance of master navigator and canoe builder Manny Sikau, from Polowat. They named the sakman "Saina," which means parent, elder, spirit, or ancestor *ti monhayon i che'cho*. A year later, the sakman was blessed and entered the waters *to sing this raised house*. The next year, the crew launched the Saina from the Hagåtña boat basin and sailed to the island of Luta, thirty-one miles north. It was the first time in centuries a sakman could be seen *flying*

By the 1890s, almost a thousand Chamorros *permanent loss* lived in Honolulu and California as part of the whaling industry. Between 1937 and 1941, the Navy recruited hundreds of Chamorros as mess attendants. The Guam Organic Act of 1950 granted Chamorros US citizenship *this cage can be either solid material wish mesh or*. In the two decades of wars in Korea

& Vietnam, thousands of Chamorro men were drafted into the military. By the 1970s, these Chamorros were scattered across various militarized US cities: San Diego, Long Beach, Vallejo, Alameda, and Fairfield *o say can you see*

1980: 30,000 Chamorros live off-island *removed from*. 1990: 50,000 Chamorros live off-island *removed from*. 2000: 60,000 Chamorros live off-island *removed from*. 2010: more of [us] live off-island than on-island. On YouTube, you can watch *red blood* Chamorros celebrating Liberation Day in *white bases* Hawai'i, California, Texas, South Carolina, Nebraska, Arizona, Nevada, Washington, Florida, and New York *blue passports*

In 2012, Traditions *map aerial and sub-aerial roots* Affirming our Seafaring Ancestry (TASA) began building a canoe house at Ypao Beach in Tumon *from multiple points of migration and return*. The canoe house will be named *because every poem is a navigational chant* Guma' Latte Marianas *because [our] bones are twenty percent water hunggan hunggan hunggan magahet ginen* tidelands *[apra harbor, guåhan] [minimum dredge depth : 49.5 feet] [turning basin : 1,092 feet radius] [channel width : 600 feet]*

once fishing
grounds—

the spanish
named it

port of san
luis de apra—

built fort santiago
over there—

fort san luis
over there—

fort santa cruz
over there—

once naval
coaling station—

dredged
after first war—

in the proposed
dredging—

veils of sediment
and silt will

plume
smolder and

shield all
light—

~

sea turtles
use natural light

cues
to navigate—

construction lights
disorient—

~

slit
habitat—

~~toninos~~
~~tanguisson~~

~~atuhong~~
~~halu'u~~

~~haggan bed'di~~
~~haggan karai~~

permanent
loss—

~

coral weaves
dead

and living
branches clusters

algae mats and
fronds across

generations to buried
coral bones—

    ⸍

to build
an artificial reef

with concrete
debris and plastic

pipes and call it
"mitigation"

    ⸍

to baptize [us]
in the turning

basin of
nuclear berth—

ginen fatal impact statements

DEIS Public Comment : "Hafa Adai! My family has a long history of serving in and in support of the US military"

> —*Hafa Adai! My family has a long history of cancer and diabetes in support of the US military*

> —*Hafa Adai! My family has a long history of dying in wars in support of the US military*

> —*Hafa Adai! My family has a long history of our land being taken in support of the US military*

> —*Hafa Adai! My family has a long history of being relocated in support of the US military*

> —*Hafa Adai! My family has a long history of forgetting in support of the US military*

DEIS Public Comment : "We were here first and I don't care if you own us. We still have a voice to say what we feel"

DEIS Public Comment : "In short, will Guam residents be relegated to 'dial-up' speeds as the military usurps the majority of available bandwidth?"

DEIS Public Comment : "Strange that no mention was made of windsurfing"

> —*The dredging of Apra will destroy a windsurfing area*

> —*Will it also destroy the wind?*

DEIS Public Comment : "I am totally against the military taking over the land at the Race Track located in Pågat"

> —*Craig, Is this an experimental translation project?*

—I read Volume Ten of the Final Environmental Impact Statement, which contains nearly all the 10,000 comments that people submitted in response to the DEIS during the official 90-day comment period

—I copy and paste phrases, sentences, words, passages from the comments of the people

—I post these comments as my Facebook status

—Sometimes others comment on the comment

—Sometimes I

ginen the legends of juan malo *[a malologue]*

⏑

from Uncle—
no matter
which Uncle—
you eat whatever
Uncle brings.

—Brandy Nālani McDougall *from* "What a Young, Single Makuahine Feeds You" (2008)

⏑

Hash is the Perfect High. That's corned beef hash for any law enforcement officer reading this. This kind of hash is not a controlled substance, but it is addictive. If you recently purchased 12-ounce cans of Hormel Corned Beef in "natural juices" on Guam, they may contain an animal de-worming drug called *ivermectin*. What's called "corned beef" is simply a poorly preserved beef imported from South America. Spread corned beef on banana leaf; overlap taro leaves; place meat in center; form a cup with taro leaves; pour in coconut milk; close leaves; fold banana leaf; tie; bake for one hour in earth oven. Note: Extremely high in fat. To reduce, replace up to half of coconut milk with whole milk. *"A coconut a day will kill you."* Hence the Chamorro special: fried rice, two eggs (any style), and one corned beef hash patty: $9.95. Conclusion: canned corned beef won't get you high, unless we're talking about your cholesterol. Simply Food, a vegetarian restaurant on Guam, serves a Soy Corned Beef. Thus, the territorialized supercedes the real. After the war, many Chamorros stayed in refugee camps and were fed salvaged Japanese rice and American excess C and D rations (corned beef and hash, powdered eggs and Navy issue coffee with cream and sugar). My grandma says it was "like manna from heaven."

ginen fatal impact statements

~

DEIS Public Comment : "That's a terrible thing to do on sacred, holy ground, and I know this because I go to Catholic school"

DEIS Public Comment : "Shame on you"

DEIS Public Comment : "This document really needs to discuss how bad traffic is going to be"

> *—Traffic is the only issue that everyone is united against*

> *—Though I'm sure there's one ultra-colonized out there who will argue that more traffic will boost the economy and preserve our culture*

> *—Parking offers structure, after all*

DEIS Public Comment : "Please don't take my grandpa's farm land away"

DEIS Public Comment : "I am a 9-year-old girl and I don't want you to do this because I love dolphins and turtles and want them to be here when I have my own kids"

DEIS Public Comment : "You are forcing us to choose between the destruction of our race, our homeland, and our culture, or to rise up against you in the hope that we may preserve something for our children and the generations to follow"

> *—hoi...I love reading these quotes you've been putting up. Gives me strength and reminds why we do the work that we do. Guaiya hao, p.s. gonna start stealing yr quotes and reposting*

ginen the legends of juan malo *[a malologue]*

When I lived in Ka'a'awa last summer with my future wife, who's Hawaiian, she seduced me with breakfasts of Corned Beef Hash, hapa rice, and two eggs (any style). For dessert, I consume her body because it's no longer a secret: canned meat *is* warrior food. Modernization, global food trade, convenience, affordability, prestige, Western economic theories of development, trapezoid cans. The rise of obesity began as imported foods from the US colonized [our] islands in the 1960s and 1970s. Their impact on the Chamorro diet chronically resonates today. I wonder how many of my relatives will carry the global burden of disease? But you know what my uncle always says: "Buy global but cook it local style!" On Sundays after mass, my grandma makes corned beef hash patties, coated with seasoned flour, fried in onions and chili, and served with white rice and two eggs (any style). Me and my brother and sister and cousins would eat without making a sound because [we] thought she stole this food from the people of the white god. But now I live in Honolulu and shop at Kokua Market, Down to Earth, and Whole Foods. Nevertheless, I have fond memories of those canned meat Sundays, my Indigenous Grandma, and her heroic efforts to make [us] believe [we] were the best fed children in all of Uncle's Empire.

[ASUELA] ::

:: [CHISEL]

ginen tidelands *[tumon, guåhan]*

~

'I Heart Guam'
si sirena—

'Western Frontier Village'
ginen barrio san nicolas—

'Island Grace'
when her mother sent her for chores—

'Hafa Adai Gun Club'
sirena enlists—

'USA Gun Club'
transformed into a fish—

'Club G Spot'
from the waist down—

'Blue House Lounge'
sirena deploys to—

'Club U.S.A. Strip Show'
sirena sees—

'Grace Massage'
it happens in the Philippines—

'Club Kamikaze'
it happens in Okinawa—

'Paradise Spa'
it happens in Hawai'i—

'Club USA Exotic Dancers'
"yangin esta unsangan, maputpumanut

'Mirage Relax Massage'
tati i fino'mu ["be careful what you ask for]

51

'Memories Massage'
hasu maulik antis di pula' i fino'mu" [once you ask for it

'You Are Here'
you can't take it back"]

ginen (sub)aerial roots

—

In 2010, I was invited by the Konsehilon Tinaotao Guam (Guam Humanities Council) to participate in the project: *8,000, How Will It Change Our Lives? Community Conversations on the US Military Buildup in Guam.* I lived the first fifteen years of my life in Guåhan *[we] have* and the last fifteen years of my life in California. My body *these excerpts* was finally returning home.

Northwest Airlines flight 635 departs from *hacha hugua tulu fatfat lima* San Francisco International Airport on March 20 at 115pm, and arrives in Tokyo at 5pm. Seat 12J. Transfer to Northwest Airlines flight 286 from Tokyo to Guam, which departs at 810pm and arrives at 1250am the next day. Seat 17F *hacha hugua tulu fatfat lima*

It was nearly midnight when the plane began descending. I took out my passport to fill in the customs declaration form *this cage can be either solid material wire mesh or* Nationality: United States of America. Place of Birth: Guam, USA. When I present the form and my passport to the customs officer, he inspects me as if I don't belong. He reads and stamps the documents without saying a word.

I will remember this moment a few years later when I arrive at the San Francisco airport from London, and the customs officer looks at my passport and says: "Hafa Adai, you're from Guam!" I reply with surprise: "Hunggan, I'm from Mongmong, but I live in Hawai'i now. What village you from?" He says: "I'm Chamorro but I grew up in California. My mom's family is from Mangilao."

When I step into the open night air, I breathe : the wind, *Puntan yan Fu'una*, their hands—*manngigne' because [our] lungs are ninety percent water*

I see the lit hotels of Tumon in the distance. After a short taxi ride, I enter the lobby of the Outrigger Hotel and notice a display that documents the construction of *Saina* and the history of TASI. From the balcony of my hotel room, I can see the shrine of San Vitores below *enemy hands pull*

At the rental car agency the next day, the sales associate asks: "Are you in the military? For the military discount." I reply: "No, but is there a discount for being Chamorro?" She says: "only if you're a Chamorro in the military."

I search an online map for directions *cues to navigate* to [our] old house in the village of Mongmong. From the Outrigger Hotel, turn right on Pale San Vitores Road. Turn left on Tumon Bay Road. Right on Marine Corps Drive. Left on Purple Heart Highway. Right on Chalan R. S. Sanchez... Even though some of the street names are different now, I remember where Uncle A, Auntie J, Charlie, and Renee used to live. I slowly pass the house. Who lives there now? *what does not change*

I continue down Chalan R. S. Sanchez until I arrive at Deboto Street *this raised house to sing*. Faded paint. A rusty storage container in the yard. Uncut grass. I want to touch the descending plumeria flowers. I want to remember everything. Yet before I can open the car door, wild dogs surround, scratching and barking—

Turn left. Reach the end of Chalan R. S. Sanchez *to avoid leaving fingerprints*. Turn left on Sergeant Roy T. Damian Jr. Street. An army specialist who was killed in the Gulf War. He was 21 years old. Turn left on Army Drive. Pass the airport. Left on Marine Corps Drive. Right on Pale San Vitores Road *this cage can be either solid material wire mesh or*. Back to the Outrigger.

–

Mangilao comes from the word *ilao: to search for something.*

The next night, I read my poetry at Meskla Chamorro Fusion Bistro. *Meskla* means *mix* or *blend*. As I look around the crowded restaurant and see many family and friends—some of whom I now remember were at the airport years ago—I finally feel like I have returned home. I only wish that my mom and dad, brother and sister (all of whom still live in various parts of California) were here—I mean there *because [our] bodies are sixty percent water hunggan hunggan hunggan magahet ginen* sounding lines *[chamorro standard time: UTC +10:00]*

                  ~

remember just
the time

-table mom made
and taped

to the fridge *when it*
is two pm here

it is eight am the next
day there—

mom always talking story
on the phone—

long distance
counting

minutes *when it*
is eleven am there

it is five pm the day
before here

her voice
transoceanic

cables
pull sounding lines

between island
and continent

when it is six pm here
it is twelve pm

the next day there—
she shows [us]

how to dial
"one six seven one

and the number"—
rotary vocal cords

pulse when
it is one am here

it is seven pm the next
day passes

into years—
fewer and fewer

calls lost
connections

avian silence—i
want to remember

when [we] once
belonged—

ginen ta(la)ya

My grandpa *o saina* struggles to tell his story. The US passed
the Guam Meritorious Claims Act in 1945. In its one-year
filing period, less than 7,000 claims were filed among 22,000
Chamorro war survivors. His voice breaks like waves *rotary vocal
chords pulse*. As part of the 1951 Peace Treaty with Japan, the
US waived wartime claims made by US citizens and nationals
against Japan. His eyes become salt *memories thread fathoms of*
water. He looks at his empty hands *to pledge allegiance*

"People in the United States need to know what [we] suffered,"
he says. Guam's first non-voting congressman to the US,
Antonio B. Won Pat, introduced a new war claims bill in
1983. The second delegate, Ben Blaz, introduced four war
claims bills, one of which would grant $20,000 for a death
claim, $5,000 for personal injury, and $3,000 for forced labor.
"At this point in my life, it's not about money—there is no
amount." The next delegate, Robert Underwood, introduced
five pieces of war claims legislation in his five terms. "I've lived
without the money for more than 60 years." Spanning nearly
20 years, none of these bills were approved by the US Congress
what follows your flag. "I just want to be heard"—

Congressman Underwood, in his last term, sought to create
a War Claims Review Commission *each thread connects [us]*
that would determine whether Chamorros were adequately
informed about *each word opens the net* and compensated by
the 1945 War Claims Act *its tides currents and depths*. The bill
passed in 2002. On December 8th and 9th, 2003, the Review
Commission held public hearings *suspended in the moment* at
which around 100 Chamorro war survivors, and relatives of
those no longer living, testified *when the net touches the water
of the page*. They spoke about the destruction of their homes
and lands, as well as to the brutality *i lahi-hu gaige giya iraq*
they witnessed or suffered. The Commission concluded that
the Chamorro people *i haga-hu gaige giya afghanistan* were
not adequately informed or compensated. Armed with this
report, Guam's next representative, Madeleine Bordallo,
introduced the Guam World War II Loyalty Recognition Act

in 2005 *i lahi-hu gaige giya iraq.* The bill sought war claims in
the amounts of $25,000 for death, $15,000 for victims who
were raped or suffered personal injury, $12,000 to those who
suffered forced labor, and $7,000 for descendants *i haga-hu
gaige giya afghanistan* of deceased survivors. Congress did not
pass the bill *o say can you see [us]*

⁓

[2008]

~~[U.S. Army Staff Sgt.~~ Joseph Gamboa ~~of the 1st Squadron,
2nd Stryker Cavalry Regiment, from Merizo died in Iraq from
injuries sustained when he came under indirect fire. He was 34]~~

~~[U.S. Army Spc.~~ Philton Ueki ~~was killed in Iraq. He was
buried in California]~~

~~[Christopher~~ Albert Quitugua ~~died in Iraq after the vehicle
he was riding in flipped after a tire blowout. He was 28]~~

~~[Guam Army National Guard Sgt.~~ Brian S. Leon Guerrero
~~was killed in Afghanistan when the vehicle he was in hit an
improvised explosive device. He was 34]~~

~~[Guam Army National Guard Spc.~~ Samson A. Mora ~~was killed
in Afghanistan when his vehicle was hit by an improvised
explosive device. He was 28]~~

~~[U.S. Navy Petty Officer 2nd Class~~ Anthony M. "Tony"
Carbullido ~~died from injuries he suffered when his convoy
vehicle hit an improvised explosive device in Afghanistan]~~

⁓

*"i believe
in the resurrection
of the*

⁓

The Department of the Navy prepared the Draft Environmental Impact Statement (DEIS) to assess the military buildup *this cage*. Released in 2009, the DEIS consisted of nine volumes and 11,000 pages *tayuyuti ham*. The community had 90 days to read, decipher, and comment *rotary vocal chords pulse*

According to the DEIS, the military planned to build their live firing range complex in an area along the northeastern coast of Guåhan *[we] have* known as Pågat, an ancestral latte village *bullets fragment and*. Many people *ricochet* travel to Pågat to fish, hike, and collect medicinal herbs; to learn about Chamorro culture and history *cues to navigate*; and to seek guidance from the ancestral spirits that dwell there *to sing future*. Pågat is also home to the Mariana eight-spot butterfly, an endangered native species *is born and fed and grows and*

‒

On Sunday, March 8, 2009, the Dulce Nombre de Maria Cathedral-Basilica in Hagåtña hosted "Operation: Special Intentions." The exhibit presented relics of St. Anthony of Padua (Patron Saint of Sailors) *tayuyuti ham*, St. Therese of Lisieux (Patron Saint of Pilots and Aircrews) *tayuyuti ham*, and St. Ignatius of Loyola (Patron Saint of Soldiers) *tayuyuti ham*. The relics arrived on Guam after a tour in Manila and then they continued to Hawai'i. Those with loved ones *my son gaige giya iraq* serving in the military were invited to enlist *my daughter gaige giya afghanistan* their names in the prayer book and to post tribute photos at the church *permanent loss*

‒

[2009]

[Hawaii Army National Guard Spc. Cwislyn K. Walter, 19, died as a result of injuries sustained in a single-vehicle accident in Kuwait]

[U.S. Army Sgt. Jasper Obakrairur, 26, of Palau, was killed by a roadside bomb in Afghanistan]

[U.S. Army 1st Sgt. Jose San Nicolas Crisostomo, formerly of Inarajan, died after an improvised explosive device detonated near his convoy in Afghanistan]

[U.S. Army Sgt. Youvert Loney, 28, from Pohnpei, died in Afghanistan, when enemy forces attacked his vehicle]

do you believe?

ginen the micronesian kingfisher *[i sihek]*

⁓

for wire enclosures
mesh size should not exceed one inch—
kingfishers have attacked

their images reflected
in glass cage fronts—these
are not legends—
the birds are
inside snake belly
[i sihek]—no
longer averting pests or
spreading
seeds—

⁓

"two of guam's endangered micronesian kingfishers were
released from quarantine at the department of agriculture.
the female birds arrived on guam about a month ago from
the philadelphia zoo (both were hatched at the st. louis zoo),
courtesy of continental airlines petsafe program *[2008] [i
sihek]*

⁓

nest logs
should be a minimum
of two feet in length with a diameter of no
less than fifteen inches—
it may be difficult to place nest logs
at this height in
captivity—*[i sihek]* the core of
the log should be exposed
so the birds have access to the soft
center *[i sihek]*
without excavating
the hard outer
bark—the national

zoo has had success using a pulley
system to lower and
raise nest
logs to check for
eggs—

~

"the saint louis zoo has hatched 41 chicks since 1985. recent
modifications to bird house habitats have now made it
possible to house *[i sihek]* a pair of these rare birds for visitors

~

what does not change / is the will

to see

ginen fatal impact statements

DEIS Public Comment : "I cannot sit back any longer. We, as a whole, need to stop being shoved around, and push back"

>*—The revolution will not be on Facebook*

>*—If it isn't on Facebook, it probably wasn't very successful*

>*—Or it was so successful that there is no more Facebook*

DEIS Public Comment : "What scares me is that I am a young female that is a target to those men who will be arriving"

DEIS Public Comment : "Thousands of horny GIs running around the island is not going to make the night life too fun, and will definitely increase the number of prostitutes on island"

DEIS Public Comment : "What if the people on Guam get outnumbered?"

DEIS Public Comment : "I request an extension of the public commenting period"

DEIS Public Comment : "And if they do take the lands that they want, then what will the meaning of Guam be?"

ginen the legends of juan malo *[a malologue]*

-

When the Spaniards returned to the ships later in the day, they brought with them the stolen skiff and a good supply of rice, fruit, and fresh water. They also carried a few buckets filled with the intestines of the slain Guamanians to be distributed among the sick as a cure for scurvy.

—Francis X. Hezel, SJ *from* The First Taint of Civilization: A History of the Caroline and Marshall Islands in Pre-Colonial Days, 1521–1885 (1994)

-

I've only shoplifted once in my life: a can of Vienna Sausages just to see if I could do it. As an altar boy, I sang tenor in the Catholic Boys Choir on Guam (the priests loved [our] little sausages). Vienna is supposed to be a city rich with culture and history, yet these sausages have none of that! North American Vienna Sausages are made from "mechanically separated" chicken finely ground to a paste and mixed with salt and spices, notably mustard, then stuffed in a long casing, cooked, after which the casings are removed. You should never serve Vienna Sausages on a first date because they are limp and soft. It's true that the sausages have an unpleasant metallic aftertaste, but that's part of the allure since my people have a long history of trading for metal. When I take my toe rings off after a long day of work, my toes swell and look like Vienna Sausages. Last night, I popped off the top of the Vienna Sausages can, drank the yummy broth, and had myself a little feast. Afterwards, I went upstairs, got my pajamas on, updated my Facebook status, and finally got a chance to lie down in bed to read some avant-garde poetry and watch some porn before bedtime. I had the most pleasant dreams.

ginen fatal impact statements

ⸯ

DEIS Public Comment : "Why Guam? Why does it have to be us?"

DEIS Public Comment : "And I still find it hard to wrap my head around everything"

DEIS Public Comment : "I feel scared because no one can tell the future"

DEIS Public Comment : "NO ACTION! But I do believe Guam needs change"

DEIS Public Comment : "The online comment box is too limiting"

DEIS Public Comment : "Why are we only limited to 2500 characters in our comments?"

> —*Do the blank spaces between words count as characters?*
> *Does silence give our words character?*

DEIS Public Comment : "Lao pa'go na ha'ane nisisita ta fanachu put i tano'ta, para i famagu'on-ta (Now is the time to stand up for our land for the future of our children)"

DEIS Public Comment : "I feel like the ko'ko' bird. My nest was on the ground. I was a flash in the forest. I took to the water"

ginen the legends of juan malo *[a malologue]*

My future wife, who's Hawaiian, prefers a Portuguese Sausage over a Vienna Sausage—if you know what I mean—but she says she'll eat anything as long as it's served with poi. On my wedding night, I hope I will be able to plump like a Ball Park Frank and not shrivel like a Vienna Sausage. Some find it suspicious that Vienna Sausage is cheaper than cat food yet marketed in disturbingly similar packaging. When Military personnel on Guam go snorkeling, they like to put Vienna sausages into Ziploc bags, take them into the water, and crumble them over the reef. Within seconds, hundreds of bright-colored tropical fish swarm like an air show. My Great Grandfather had mouth cancer so he would mash Vienna Sausages and mix them with rice pudding. My Grandfather would mash Vienna Sausages and make them into a sandwich with white bread and mayonnaise. My dad eats Vienna Sausage as a "chaser" with his Budweiser. Yet I am not ashamed because somewhere on the Western coast of the United States, a shirtless Chamorro suffering from a severe case of diaspora is kicking back with his Budweiser and can of Vienna Sausages saying, "Ah, this tastes just like home!"

[KANNAI] ::

:: [HAND]

ginen the micronesian kingfisher *[i sihek]*

~

—of trespass—*[i sihek]*

when land is
caged [we]

—of theft—*[i sihek]*

are caged within
[our] disappearance

~

"a mated pair of guam micronesian kingfishers...laid two
fertile eggs this spring deep inside a hollowed-out palm
log in a special breeding room of the lincoln park zoo bird
house. keepers promptly stole one of the eggs...the parents
incubated and hatched one egg in the hollow log...the other
egg hatched [a few days later] inside an incubation machine in
a lab, where the chick now lives, fed by keepers from tweezers
protruding beneath the beak of an oversized kingfisher hand
puppet *[2010]*

[i sihek]

~

invasion is
a continuous chain of
immeasurably destructive
events in time—

is the death of *[i sihek]*
origins—
is a stillborn *[i sihek]*
future—is the ending of
all nests this
choked thing [we] *[i sihek]*

~

what does not change / is the will to colonize

~

as weapons
mount—   *[i sihek]*

risk
being Chamoru   *[i sihek]*

rise
above fences   *i sihek*

ginen ta(la)ya

~

My second book of poems was published in 2010, coinciding with my trip home for the Humanities Council. My publisher (based in California) shipped boxes of my book across the ocean. While on-island, I shared my poetry with students at various public high schools *where fish are biting*. At one school I see *depending on the angle of the sun* a life-sized cardboard cutout of a uniformed soldier carrying a machine gun, standing perfectly still *surface movement of currents and shadows*. Recruiters stalk *ghost nets*

~

[2010]

{U.S. Army Spc. Eric M. Finniginam, 26, of Yap, died of wounds sustained when insurgents attacked his unit in Afghanistan}

{U.S. Army Sgt. Joshua Akoni Sablan Lukeala, 23, formerly of Yigo, died while in combat in Afghanistan}

{U.S. Marine Cpl. Dave Michael Santos, 21, was killed in Afghanistan}

{Army Pfc. Jaysine "Jen" Petree, 19, was killed by an improvised explosive device in Afghanistan}

~

please help
[us]
find guam

~

I drive alone *avian silence* to the Guam International Airport, which is designed to resemble an outrigger canoe. The airport is located in Tiyan *land theft permanent loss*. Tiyan translates as *belly* or *breadbasket*. As I walk towards the departure gate, I see twenty-three banners : "The Fallen Brave of Micronesia." Name, rank, flag *shields all light*. The dedication ceremony for this *cage can be either solid material wire mesh or* pictorial memorial occurred in 2007 as an official event of the Liberation Day festivities. I see the banner honoring Jonathan Santos. If I ever write a novel, I say to him, I will name a character after you *this choked thing [we]*

Northwest Airlines flight 773 departs *hacha hugua tulu fatfat lima* from Guam International Airport on April 3 at 1010am and arrives in Tokyo at 1255pm. Seat 16G. Transfer to Northwest flight 634, which departs from Tokyo at 340pm and arrives in San Francisco at 905am the same day. Seat 12A *hacha hugua tulu fatfat lima*

~

My grandpa, like many others of his generation, joined the US military after the war *his uniform*. After being stationed abroad for many years, he returned to Guam and worked for the National Park Service War Memorial. "My job was to preserve things that I wasn't willing to build in the first place," he says.

Congress established Guam's War in the Pacific National Historical Park in 1978. The commemorative park consists of seven parcels of land *invasion is* throughout the island, each representing *a continuous chain of* an aspect of the battle. The signage of the park, originally in *enemy tongues* English and Japanese, told tales of heroic American liberators, stoic Japanese soldiers, and loyal Chamorro victims *buried coral bones*. Around 1,000 Chamorros died during the war. Of the 22,000 who survived, less than 1,000 are alive today *hands remain empty to be heard*

~

I was 17 years old when the recruiter *of trespass of theft* visited [our] house in California. I was 21 years old when the US invaded Afghanistan. I was 23 years old when the US invaded

Iraq. If we enlist *as weapons mount* to pay [our] debt of liberation, what are [our] bodies worth?

The average death claim paid in the 1945 Guam Claims Acts was about $1,900 dollars *coral weaves dead and living*. If the deceased was 12 years old or *eggs and larvae* younger: $500. For each additional *relics and rosaries* year up to age 21: add $500 with *laces thread empty boots* a maximum of $5,000. For each additional year *when [we] once belonged* up to age 61: subtract $100. If older than 61 years: $1,000 flat *empty hands mannginge' with [our] entire breath*

~

The War in the Pacific Memorial Wall was *a cage can be either solid material wire mesh or* completed in 1994. The wall panels include the names of civilians and soldiers who suffered and *is born and fed and grows and* died during the war. A list of known names was compiled and printed as an insert *o say can you see [us]* in the local newspaper. The public verified and added to the list. The newspaper insert was also circulated to off-island Chamorro organizations *rotary vocal chords echo location*. The original list was updated, reprinted in the newspaper, and circulated twice more. In total: 16,142 names *map trauma*. Since 1996, more than a hundred more names have surfaced *because our eyes are ninety percent water*

~

Instead of the military buildup and the DEIS choking [our] voices, it ignited an underwater volcano *these passages my sourcing*. Chamorros on-island and off-island [our] *stories cast upon the intertidal zone* mobilized, protested, and spoke out against the buildup [our] *stories weave generations this raised house to sing*

When I see my grandpa *stand in the tide* after my first book was published, he places his hand *to gather [our] net of words* on my shoulder and says, "No one can take our story from us." I don't remember if he ever let go *because [our] skin is forty percent water hunggan hunggan hunggan magahet*

75

ginen sounding lines

[for my mom]

⁓

"don't swim by yourself when
you're back home

be careful in the ocean
many beaches are polluted now

just swim in the agana pool
remember that's where you learned

and your dad was happiest
when he was swimming laps—

⁓

please take a few minutes
to complete the questions below

this information helps us
understand visitors to guam

and ensures your experience remains
the best it can be—

⁓

"your dad can't swim now
with his bad back and legs

no we don't like the pool here
at the new apartment

and your dad got a rash after
he swam in the pool

at the veterans center
in san jose—

~

my last trip to guam was
this trip to guam is my

where i/we
plan to stay while on guam is

i am a returning
guam resident

an intended resident moving
to guam for longer than 90 days

a visitor—

~

"i hope there's no water outage
when you're home

remember filling the tubs
sinks and pots during typhoons

i'll never forget that one strong typhoon
we boarded the windows but the rain

still flooded the bedrooms
so we put our pillows and blankets

in the hallway and closed
all the doors and slept

all night the rain and
winds never stopped

but [we] were safe
together—

          ~

the primary reason
for this trip to guam is

holiday sight-seeing relaxation
gold diving business

adventure medical treatment
sports related educational

english language test
tour wedding honeymoon

convention conference
employment government shopping

school excursion military
other—

          ~

"remember it was raining
the night we landed in san francisco

hopefully it won't rain tomorrow
your dad will drive you to the airport

just remember to drink lots of water
on the long flight home—

The Southbank Centre, a London arts organization, invited me to represent Guam at Poetry Parnassus, a weeklong "Cultural Olympiad" that featured a poet from each of the countries competing in the 2012 Olympics.

I flew from Honolulu (where I now live) to San Francisco for an eight-hour layover before the connecting flight to London. My sister, Marla, picks me up from the airport to meet my mom, dad, and brother, Brian, at a nearby seafood restaurant to talk story for a few hours. Before I return to the airport, my dad gives me a bag of chicken kelaguen to eat on the flight. My mom gives me an envelope of money and whispers, "for chenchule'."

After arriving at the London airport, I give the customs declaration form and passport to the customs officer. "You're American," he says. I reply, "No, I'm not American, but I'm a US citizen." Then I explain what a "Guam" is.

~

Mongmong comes from the word *momongmong, the sound of a heartbeat*. The scene from Helen Perez's story, "Bittersweet Memories," ends: "[My friend] knelt down next to me and we looked really carefully and finally she said, 'Here it is, see this little dot, it says Guam, USA.' I stared and leaned closer to get a good look, and there it was, just a tiny dot on this big map" *because [our] blood is eighty percent water hunggan hunggan hunggan magahet.*

ginen tidelands *[pågat, guåhan]*

~

"Prutehi yan Difendi"

—Bernadita Camacho-Dungca *from* "Inifresi" (1991)

~

o saina
hu ufresen

~

i tano'
i kottura

~

live fire
munitions in

~

i aire
i manglo'

~

cross aim
target island

~

i napu
i hinengge

~

this web
of caves

~

i ababang
i latte

~

bullets fragment
and ricochet

~

pågat means
to speak

~

o saina
hu ufresen

~

i tasi
i lengguåhi

~

guaha means
to exist

~

o saina
hu ufresen

hanom #ourislands hanom aresacred hanom

~

from sourcings

from the legends of juan malo

—Juan Malo is a young, poor Chamorro man who lived in Guåhan during Spanish colonial occupation. His mischievous adventures (reminiscent of other indigenous tricksters) involved outwitting and deceiving the Spanish governor and other officials with the help of his karabao (water buffalo). In Spanish, *malo* means *bad*. The "malologues" included in this collection are dedicated to Juan's spirit of resistance.

—In 2010, the Guam Legislature passed a bill officially changing the name of "Guam" to "Guåhan."

from (sub)aerial roots

—I am indebted to several articles on Guampedia for information on latte stones: "Latte's Significance," by Fred Rodriguez; "Latte Structures," by Lawrence J. Cunningham; and "Latte" by Rosalind L. Hunter-Anderson.

—Helen Perez's story, "Bittersweet Memories," can be found in *Chamoru Childhood* (Achiote Press, 2009), edited by Victoria Leon-Guerrero, Michael Lujan Bevacqua, and Craig Santos Perez. Helen is my mom, and she claims that I inherited all my writing talents from her.

—I am indebted to Selina Onedera-Salas for the grammar lesson, which appeared on Facebook.

—I am indebted to Robert Underwood, Faye Untalan, Michael Perez, and Jesi Lujan Bennett for their scholarship on Chamorro migration and diaspora.

—In Chamorro custom, mannginge' is an expression of deep respect: bow towards and touch your nose to the back of an elder's hand. Breathe in.

—In 1989, the Guam International Airport was renamed the "Antonio B. Won Pat International Airport."

—The story of the sakman is a recasting of a story from my second book, *from unincorporated territory [saina]*.

—When I was packing to move from California to Hawai'i in 2010, I found an old writing journal. Hidden in its pages were three photos, time stamped "1995," that I had completely forgotten about. The pictures were of my first and only visit to Pågat.

—In Chamorro custom, chenchule' refers to a gift and the act of giving. It is usually practiced at special events, or at the beginning of a journey. If you receive chenchule', you accept the responsibility to reciprocate.

from ta(la)ya

—The headline "US Territories: A Recruiter's Paradise: Army Goes Where Fish Are Biting" is from the *Salt Lake Tribune* (8/05/07).

—The names of the soldiers were retrieved online from a feature in the *Pacific Daily News* titled "Remembering our Fallen," posted on May 2, 2011, as well as from the Office of Insular Affairs website, under "Fallen Insular Heroes."

—I am indebted to Keith Camacho, Michael Lujan Bevacqua, Vince Diaz, Lisa Natividad, Gwen Kirk, and David Hanlon for their scholarship on Liberation Day, Chamorro soldiers, the history and religiosity of militarization on Guåhan, and war claims legislation in Micronesia. I am indebted to Victoria Leon-Guerrero for her article "The War Reparations Saga: Why Guam's Survivors Still Await Justice," posted on the website Guam War Survivor Story. I am also indebted to the scholarship of H. D. K. Herman on the War in the Pacific National Park.

—The story about my grandpa is a recasting of a story from my first book, *from unincorporated territory [hacha]*.

—Jonathan Pangelinan Santos joined the army after high school. He was deployed to Iraq in 2004. They nicknamed him "The Librarian" because he collected books in Iraq. He also kept a written and video diary. He wrote: "I will read 'The Principles of Writing,' and then I will write the Great American novel and get hired as a professor at a prestigious university" ("'The Corporal's Diary': Fallen Soldier's Journal and Videotapes Inspire Documentary," by Donald Allen, in *Stars and Stripes*, 1/4/09). In 2008, documentary filmmaker Patricia Boiko produced and codirected "The Corporal's Diary: 38 Days in Iraq," which features Jonathan's words and video footage. Jonathan was 22 years old when he was killed in Iraq.

ginen tidelands *[tumon, guåhan]*

—The first lines of each couplet are signs I saw in Tumon, Guam's main tourist village.

ginen sounding lines *[chamorro standard time: UTC +10:00]*

—The "Chamorro time zone" observes standard time by adding ten hours to coordinated universal time (UTC+10). The zone is two hours behind Wake Island time zone, fifteen hours ahead of North American Eastern time zone, and seventeen to eighteen hours ahead of the Pacific time zone. The Chamorro time zone was established by public law 106-564 (2000), legislated by the US Congress.

~

ginen the micronesian kingfisher *[i sihek]*

—The quoted passages in this poem are excerpted and edited from press releases and articles on the Smithsonian National Zoo, San Diego Zoo, Philadelphia Zoo, and Saint Louis Zoo websites. The last quoted passage is from the article "One of the World's Most Endangered Species, Guam Kingfishers Live on in Zoos in Struggle to Survive," by William Mullen (*Chicago Tribune*, 6/27/10).

—Because zookeepers were not familiar with Micronesian kingfisher diets, they fed them newborn mice. Some birds confused their blind and naked hatchlings with food.

—According to the *Micronesian Kingfisher Species Survival Plan: Husbandry Manual (Halcyon cinnamomina cinnamomina)*, edited by Beth Bahner, Aliza Baltz and Ed Diebold (1998), the Guam Bird Rescue Project (initiated in 1984) captured 29 Micronesian kingfishers and transferred them to US zoos for captive breeding. The current population descends from these birds. The last wild birds were seen on Guåhan in 1988.

~

ginen fatal impact statements

—To read the Environmental Impact Statement for the military buildup, see: www.guambuildupeis.us/ documents. For more information on militarization, see the Militarization in the Marianas website (www.milmarianas. com/index.html).

Guinaya

This book is dedicated to [our] Chamoru creators, Puntan and Fu'una, ancestral brother and sister, and to all my ancestors who continue to give me strength and hope that someday [our] people will truly be liberated. *Saina Ma'ase.*

This book is dedicated to all my Micronesian brothers and sisters who have died while serving the US military, and to all the families who have lost loved ones.

This book is dedicated to my mom, dad, brother, and sister. Even though [we] no longer live in the same house, you are always in my heart. This book, and my life, would not have been possible without your love. *Saina Ma'ase.*

This book is dedicated to the group *We Are Guåhan* and to all those at home and in the diaspora who spoke out against the military buildup in Guåhan and the Mariana Islands. *Saina Ma'ase.*

~

This book is dedicated to Brandy Nālani McDougall, my heart, my everything. I am excited to share a life full of poetry and other intimate collaborations with you. Mahalo for welcoming me to your home islands and for building a new home with me. *Hu guaiya hao.*

~

Thanks to Kimberlee Kihleng and all the folks at the Guam Humanities Council for bringing me home. Thanks to Anna Selby of Poetry Parnassus for inviting me to represent my home in London. *Saina Ma'ase.*

Thanks to Susan Schultz and Tinfish Press, who believed in my first book. Thanks to Richard Hamasaki and Doug Matsuoka for amplifying my voice in the poetry album,

Undercurrent. Endless thanks to my current editors, Rusty Morrison and Ken Keegan and the entire Omnidawn crew, for your continued support of this project. Thanks, Rusty, for giving this book its ocean-ready form. And thanks, Cassie, for giving this book its design to carry the winds. *Saina Ma'ase.*

Thanks to the Ethnic Studies graduate program at the University of California, Berkeley, for supporting my academic research during the writing of this book—especially faculty member Beth Piatote. Thanks to the faculty and students of the English Department at the University of Hawai'i, Mānoa. Mahalo for welcoming me into the department and giving me a supportive space to complete this project. *Saina Ma'ase.*

Thanks to the passionate educators who have taught my books in your classrooms, and who have invited me to speak at your schools and engage with your students. Thanks, also, to all the brilliant scholars who have reviewed and written essays about my work. *Saina Ma'ase.*

Thanks to all the editors who published versions of these poems over the years in scholarly and literary, online and print journals: *Amerasia Journal*; *The Journal of Transnational American Studies*; *Socialism Capitalism Nature*; *Taos Journal of Poetry and Art*; *Cordite Poetry Review*; *Trout*; *The Brooklyn Rail*; *Cura: A Literary Magazine of Art and Action*; *PEN Poetry Series*; *Platte Valley Review*; *Amerarcana: A Bird and Beckett Review*; *Altered Scale*; *Huihui: Pacific Rhetoric and Aesthetics*; *Conversations at the Wartime Café: A Decade of War 2001–2011*; *Jubilat*; *P-Queue*; *The Offending Adam*; *Storyboard*; *Indigenous Writers from Micronesia*; *Tinfish*; and *Doveglion*.

~

This book is for you, dear reader. As gift, as *chenchule'*.

~